Myth Opportunities

by Peter Lechuga
Cover Art and Illustrations
by Jannette Alejandra Lopez

Advance Praise for
Myth Opportunities

"Peter Lechuga is a Chicano author that shapes words like obsidian – sharp and transparent about his heritage. His writing flows with the rhythm of brown American blues, capturing the heart of Chicano identity, struggle and resilience."

- Ceasar K. Avelar, Poet Laureate of Pomona, author of *God of the Air Hose and Other Blue-Collar Poems*

"Myth Opportunities is for the word seekers. The hip-hop heads. A book for the poetry nerds who don't mind being given swirlies of word play, who don't mind being left inside of lockers of myths, storytelling, and poetry."

- Alma Rosa Azul, owner of Barrio Fuerza, author of *Mariaposa*

"Peter Lechuga's *live* poetry performances are both captivating and inspiring; MYTH OPPORTUNITIES allows his audience to take that fire home, not only in their spirits, but in their hands! Lechuga dives into devastating details of self-analysis and environmental scrutiny. This debut is a rush of love, religion, history, politics, and personal confession cascading in vivid colors. The reds are bloody;

the yellows blaze! Lechuga's language is original and brilliantly volcanic.

- Sondria Bailey, author of *The Carverians* series

"Peter Lechuga's new poetry collection *Myth Opportunities* blends this incredible world of indigenous and Greek mythology with his contemporary life. With stellar use of rhythm, unique rhyme patterns and intriguing imagery, Peter invites the reader into real, raw, experiences. "For those who chew lightbulbs to dwell in the dark", he does not shy away from the messiness that comes with honest storytelling, whether the subject is family, religion, or injustice. Although, the collection is peppered with delightful, yet thoughtful gems like his tea haikus."

- J.E. Coats, author of *Midnight and Mad Dreams*

"Peter Lechuga is redefining the poetry game and shaping the way we view culture, words and what it means to be human in an utterly chaotic and clustered society."

- Niño from the Block, find him at Liam's on Monday nights belting out karaoke bangers

"*Myth Opportunities* is a tantalizing opportunity for the reader to join the writer on a lyrical time travel journey from myths of the great Aztec empire era to the legendary modern-day lowriders. Sprinkled in are deep, cultural customs of indigenous people creating a virtual epic. Rich in verbal virtuosity that can only be truly appreciated with a great cultural awareness of the indigenous native people of the land and a good dictionary. Garnished with the personal experiences of the author, both bitter and sweet, will leave most readers sated yet wanting more. A recommended read for those who read in colors and/or shapes, not just words.

- Ernst Fenelon Jr., facilitator of the Prison Education Project, poet and author of *Three Things that Everybody Wants to Know About You and the Five Step Plan for Life Success*

"*Myth Opportunities* is that 'brujeria through a boombox' you've been searching for, a thumping brew bubbling over its cauldron and boiling down into the roots of the earth, amplifying nature's voice into a beat everyone can moan and dance to. Through ruined parties and surreal gardens, Lechuga draws connections between ancient Greek revelry and contemporary Chicano sadness, between Holy Eucharist and Gaia, between protest chants and the Fifth Sun. Lechuga believes in the pulsating power of the eternal now, all while making you painfully aware of just how naked grief can leave you, and how comforting a few too many glasses of numbness can be."

- David Romero, Co-founder of El Martillo Press, author of *Diamond Bars 2*

"*Myth Opportunities* is Peter's powerful debut poetry collection, where indigenous spirits come alive through vivid storytelling. With an evocative blend of culture, identity, and love, Peter's poems invite you to journey into realms of raw emotion, ancestral memory, and personal reflection woven into every line. Each page pulses with imagery that leaps from the page, making words dance and connect to universal truths. Peter's lyrical voice bridges the past and present, creating a profound narrative that resonates with the strength and resilience of their heritage. *Myth Opportunities* is an invitation to immerse yourself in a world where tradition meets the contemporary."

- Chai Savathasuk, author of *How Chai Tea is Made*

"Peter Lechuga, author of Myth Opportunities, is a man of honor, truth, love and respect for self. He's a poet who unfolds his vulnerability page-to-page exposing his tenderness and courage. Skillfully detailed, he strategically and creatively plants every word to be remembered like an echo of fresh breath. Each page is beautifully exquisite like the perfect sip of moonlight tea. *From Home to Home of Stone Turned into Dust Horizon* was my absolute favorite. '*While blood and smoke lick the sky,*' I love the imagery. Peter's tongue beats a frequency connecting to the sacred fire of being human. *Constellations* was a beautiful and powerful story between mother, son, and loss. This book, this lifeline was and is absolutely phenomenal.

- VOTH | Voice of the Harbor, author of *Dieagnosis*

Myth Opportunities
© 2024 Peter Lechuga
ISBN:978-1-966337-03-4

Cover art:
© 2024, Jannette Alejandra Lopez

First Edition, 2024

All rights reserved. No part of this publication may be reproduced, distributed, or
transmitted in any form or by any means, including photocopying, recording, or
other electronic or mechanical methods, without the prior written permission of the
publisher, except in the case of brief quotations embodied in critical reviews and
certain other noncommercial uses permitted by copyright law.

Printed in the United States of America

Edited by Peter Lechuga
Cover Design by Janette Alejandra Lopez
Layout Design by Erica Castro

For my family and loved ones that are no longer on this plane.
For my muse, my darling, Alejandra.
For my mother.

Foreword

This collection by Peter Lechuga is an expansive cliff note into the ethos of a conscious Mexican American. Conscious of who he has ancestrally been and who he must wholly and holistically become.

From colorful Haiku to historical slant rhyme mixed with muti-lingual alliteration. This collection of poetry is an exposé of language and inner character as well as communal response and responsibility.

Peter Lechuga is calling for a response from our spirits.

- David "Judah 1" Oliver, First Poet Laureate of Pomona, founder of LionLike Mindstate, author of *WHILE SEATED.*, *Child of the Sun. Man of the Moon*, and *Instructions for Alchemy.Ingredients of Ether.*

xii

Table of Contents

Preface   xvii

I. I Still Worship the Sun

Xochimiquitzli	5
Mythconception	6
Chicano Dionysus	8
Make Myth	11
Haikus pt.1	13
I Don't Realize	15
From Home of Home to Stone Turned into	
Dust Horizon	16
Keep Crafting	19
Home is Never Ogygia	20
Mare Icarium	21
Tletl	23
Rub the Soil on your Soul	24
Speak Sibylline	26
I Bump in the Night	27
Karaoke Night in the Underworld	29
Stain my Skin	30
Sitting in St. Ferdinand's	31
Never Hide	36
Dear Elpenor,	37
Reverse Nervous	39
Mictēcacihuātl,	41
East and West	43

II. I Drink Tea Now

The Perfect Tea	49
I Met an Artist from Pomona	51
Two Statues in a Garden	52
My Eyes Caught You and I Thought	53
Haikus pt. 2	55

Snapping	58
How To Train a Tiger	60
Our First Kiss Lies in the Spring of Yesterday	61
My Love Language is	62

III. Family Fables

See Ya', Sofia	67
My Mother is a Hummingbird	70
Hand-Me-Down	78
Mom's Kitchen	80
Constellations	82
Tonāntziné	87
End	
Acknowledgements	91
About the Author	95

xv

xvi

Preface

Growing up, my mother would create these fantastic worlds in bedtime stories. The silliest characters would make the mundane feel spectacular as they accomplished the most phenomenal feats. I would struggle futilely, fighting my heavy eyelids to hear more and more. I would dream of these stories nightly as they pressed their warmth upon my head and even now that warmth still lingers. My mother taught me the power of words, the weight stories carry and that is where my love of storytelling and writing was born.

As a young Catholic, with early doubts brewing, I wanted to learn more about what other people believed. What if what I was taught wasn't all there was or correct? From this point, I dove into mythology and never turned back. In my teens, I turned to the Greeks and discovered their impact on western culture and the art of storytelling itself, I was enamored. As I continued to read about other cultures' histories and religions, I eventually learned about my own ancestors and what they believed. The powerful Azteca gods my people feared and worshipped, until their beliefs and land were colonized and Catholicism was seared onto their minds and tongues due to the diseases these white saviors exhaled with their halitosis and lies. I felt lost between two worlds. Should I worship the Fifth Sun or the bearded, blue-eyed son?

This book is broken into three parts. In the first, I pour my beliefs on the page, as the worlds of the religion I was born into, mythology, and the spirits of my ancestors coalesce into poems about carving out your own myth and forging your own path. I have lost many loved ones along my journey and I honor their impact on the world by telling their stories and just a piece of the legacy they have left behind.

I am a romantic and truly none of this would be possible without my beautiful partner supporting me and pushing me forward through the most challenging of times. The second part in this collection is dedicated to her and her love of tea which includes some love poems I have written throughout the years. She has shaped this lifelong coffee addict into a fledgling tea connoisseur, who is just beginning to learn all he can about this herbal world.

The final part is stories of my family and my experiences growing up adopted, confused, and riddled with Catholic guilt. My family is important to me and without them, I never would have found my passion and the strength to persevere.

With this collection I want to express that we are currently creating myths for the future. So, I implore each of us to look within and find our own greatness and story to tell. Share it with the world. Every opportunity is a Myth Opportunity.

xix

xx

Myth Opportunities

2 |

I.
I Still Worship the Sun

4 |

Xochimiquiztli

In ritual war, boys held their clubs tight
and high into the wide sky. Jagged black
teeth, buried in wood, were licked clean by light
after they chewed flesh off other boys' backs.

Weapons hungered like roaring bellies, flames
of sacred forest blessed breath. Young bodies
dragged slowly, they watched rivals do the same.
Brothers floating through fields of red poppies

remembered in chipped glass and bright, ruby
hummingbird throats. Captives sang of flowers;
words became petals dancing with duty.
Fate be fed; warriors never cower.

Taste the blood and carve the heat of the sun
from their chests; the obsidian and jade
eat for gods. We still sacrifice our sons
to famished symbols. An offering made:

Mi abuelo his legs, my dad his knees.
Mi padrino… no flowery death among the trees.

Mythconception

I am from lowriders hittin' switches
and peacocks struttin' on the lawns of old missions
I am from masa harina flung at the wall
I am from Tláloc speaking in thunder and rainfall
I am from sacred shoes, divine, blemishes and all

I am from sci-fi novels and Russian lit
I am from West Coast hip hop
and Scribble Jam vids
I am from witch-hazel thriving in the hills ageless
I am from creaking church pews
and bibles with gilded pages

I am from earthquakes and water rations
I am from the Fifth Sun burning with our passions
I am from an adoptive family whose love
is the kindest I've ever known
I am from a pen, a pad, and a poem

Chicano Dionysus

I used to be a Dionysus.
When I was younger, I'd watch all mi tíos drink,
lose
control of their bodies.
Limp limbs swinging
like the lives of the parties
they were.

I wanted to be them.

Oldies booming,
look how they
transform.
Arms grooving
with a beer
glass or
machismo oozing
all on the
dance floor.

I used to be a Dionysus.
When I got older, I'd watch mi tíos drink, lose
control of their bodies.
Limp limbs dangling,
a colostomy bag to potty.
Last drink
in an IV drip.

I still remember them

tripping
off-beat to *La Chona*.
Sipping
endless bottles of Coronas.
They'd leave glass mountain plots
in their wake.
Years later we'd take fountains of shots
by their graves.

I used to be a Dionysus.
Now, I watch mi amigos drink, lose
control of their cars.
Limp limbs lying lifeless in the dark.

I will never forget them

being eighty-six'd
from every bar.
Killing twelve packs
then shredding on guitar.
You were so excited
about your new pedal.
If only I could fight it,
keep you away from that pedal.

I used to be a Dionysus
but here on out, I simply refuse
to watch waning moons blur
into beating suns.
I've found it's truly not worth

losing yourself or the ones you love.

Maenads mitote so vividly.
Broken bottles bleed out fragility.
I used to be a Dionysus;
however,
I abdicate my divinity.

Make Myth

Brillo mas, brillo mas.
Historia es sagrada; tu entras.

Brillo mas, brillo mas.
Historia es sagrada.

Animalistic traditions sewn in bones
that don't break.
We're of jaguars, not of fish,
so, we'll never take the bait.

Tie the Sol around our waists,

fly with feathers of our faith.
Emerald into blue, a changing view,
awaken a new fate

All empires crumble
under a drunken white god's stumble.
A savior's sins diseased they breathe
and oh are we in trouble.
Bury them so slow and deep,
low beneath the rubble
so, we can sing a chorus high
but keep our voices humble.

Notes danced around a holy pyre,
shining bright deeply.
Ancient hums turned into hymns

and we are fed christ weekly.
Communion,
a union
of celestial and human.
Reunion
of the Earth and sky into a sweet infusion

And I drink…
And I bleed…
And I think…

We're noble beasts of bone & dust painted upon a
chart.
We proudly look upon ourselves, each time we
gaze at stars.
I'll slash my burning belly to offer all my heart,
a beating drum of flesh and blood displayed as
perfect art.

And I drink…
And I bleed…
And I think…

Brillo mas, brillo mas.
Historia es sagrada; tu entras.

Brillo mas, brillo mas.
Historia es sagrada.
La communidad es sagrada.
Mi gente es sagrada.

Left-Handed Hummingbird

I watch you war, as
the sky burns bright a new sun.
You turn night to day.

Two Rabbit

The color of milk
scalds tongues and cascades down to
sit on smiling hearts.

Smoking Mirror

Dark desires are held
in an obsidian pool
destiny awaits

Full of Sores

A sacrifice must
be made. I humble myself
before famished flame.

Moon

Where the rabbit sleeps
above, we see ears dancing
in the glowing light.

Precious Twin

Hurricanes spiral
as jewels gleam from your chest.
Knowledge rides the wind.

I Don't Realize

when I'm anxious I pick at my skin.
wishing I could shed it like the thin,
split-tongued serpent who fed us sin
in a garden. I'd like to thank him

for defiling paradise, because now fruit
tastes sweet and lust does too.
Nectar sticks to lips and the roof
of my impure mouth. Deep roots

of apocrypha grow thick and far
into our wooden spines. On stars,
some wish. I pray to the constellations of scars
on your alabaster legs. With my heart

I worship your celestial body. Blood
and hips that float on my lap through floods
and revelation. I mask my face in mud
then lie in turned soil to let the flower buds

grow over guilt and gloom. It begins,
when I'm anxious I pick at my skin.

From Home to Home of Stone Turned into Dust Horizon

Are we destined to run?
To live out these diaspora days from now
until the end has come?

And what is the end?
When the gates of Aztlan swing open
and we return in droves,
as the Fifth Sun finally explodes?
Exhaling its last
breath of warmth and light?
An open palm flash of white heat
closing into a brown fist?
While blood and smoke lick the sky,
like a lover dragging their tongue
upon the body they find most sacred?
If the horizon holds only weeping clouds
floating as withered crowns,
scraped by steel,
then I am sick of running.

Spit from my throat,
I draw the thirsting sword I sheathed long ago.
A hilt of red silt and bone,
blooming blade of burning palo santo,
drinking the sweat off our backs
and the salt from our tired eyes.
Fear these wild arms as they strike the night,
like the stretching branches

of a great oak.
If history is written by the victors,
then I promise our hearts
and hands will write forever.
Through cramp and crook,
quill pens made from clay feathers
will drain the claret of our oppressors.

No monuments of metal,
no blights of great height,
no crushers of culture are wanted.
You see...
Silver prison hollow
tries to follow us,
erase what's hallowed, trust
that all will rust
and bend easier than our wills.
Our skin is of the soil on which we stand.
The dangling roots on our soles bravely dig into the
future
while they lovingly grip onto the past.

Beneath us is a burial ground,
where the spirits speak in stereo sound.

You are hearing them now.
You are hearing them now.

Don't run.

18 | I Still Worship the Sun

Keep Crafting

in the turquoise lake and glade.
Recall how the feathered serpent of jade
has his jeweled eye displayed

shining in true north. Rejoice
that he blessed the wind with voice
so, we could produce noise

to summon sweet song
and bleed blistering art along
the streets. Never get it wrong

our hands are made to create,
our minds are made to shake
the foundation.

Home is Never Ogygia

For those who chew lightbulbs
to dwell in the dark,
do you sit lotus-legged in the bleak gloom
and gnaw on the black flowers and honeyed fruit
with drool gleaming on your doomed
glass smiles and chipped teeth?
Gaslight while lips bleed;
masks tight in deceit.

The light is on
and no one wants to be home.

Mare Icarium

When the cage creaked
open and the dule of doves lifted
their weighted wings,
It was clear they couldn't ascend
above the tree line.
So much for the peace they'd bring.

If those doves actually represented you,
they'd Icarus themselves and watch
as their white plumes char
into greying ash. They'd feel their wax beaks
melt into their brains
and spend the moment they had left in this life
remembering the good times.

Your family would be Daedelus
but they would hang
their flush faces down
in embarrassment
and leave your corpse
discarded to drown
in the shallow gutter
where that car hit you.

That's when I learned how deep
a puddle could be.
Hopelessly crimson and vast

as it transformed into the sea
where you were lost
forever.

Who mourns the forgotten?
Who spares them loose change?
Who trusts their pleas?
Who cares?

I glance again at the doves
and exhale relief to see their feathers
have not been burnt black.
I'm happy that today
they couldn't fly
into the sun.

Tletl

In every language flames
burn the same.

Stoves, kindling, hills, cars, buildings.

The tongues don't ask to tango,
they just dance.

Rub the Soil on your Soul

Outer darkness
Out of sight
Daughters harness
Inner light

Cosmic promise
Weight of life
Karmic vomit
Empty night

You can't control
so, mind your sole
purpose.
read divine curses
scribbled, fine cursive
redefines wordless.
Feeling quite nervous?
Where are the bodies
of those they find worthless?
I ask where do they hide the bodies?

Mined coal soul crushed cold
stagnant black water.
Bloodshed fed to lambs' heads
bred for slaughter.
I'll lay it out
without a doubt.
What you wish will trickle down
is not about to spout,

we're in a drought

Prophet sharing
Words slurred
often staring
blurred nerves
coffin pairings
Served first
caustic heirs bring
murder

Amendments weren't found in shining glow
on Sinai plateau.
Not written in stone
or scriptural tome;
they were chiseled on bones
of those ripped from their homes.
Dismissed all alone.
Left to traverse the mists of unknown.
We were the first to fight the worst of their chrome.

So let it be known...

Speak Sibylline

Tilt our heads back,
pour the ambrosia of rotting grapes
into our craving slack
jaws. The rancid wine overflows as it paints

our confused, swinging necks
red; heads hang heavy like
sunflowers at dusk. What's next?
For the blood, it never dries

but hollow bodies of water do.
Fish in desolate beds writhe
as we lose a source of food.
How's one to survive

if we can't trust the truth?
How's our soul to rise
if our husk is constantly abused?
Apanohuaia, hear my cries

and allow me to be baptized
by you.

I Bump in the Night
(previously published in The Chaffey Review vol. 18)

all the tunes
that my ghosts love.
Genre phases like the moon,
spinning wax up above.

Jamming to hip-hop and punk,
ska and some indie picks,
dub, jazz, oldies, funk
and finish with those Jimi riffs.

I turn the fucking bass up
and let that woofer bark.
Homies shake off the grave dust,
break the quiet of the dark.

This a seance on speakers,
brujeria through a boombox,
a party in the ether,
afterlife interlude spot.

I've had too many friends,
too young, pass to the unknown
but when I play their favorite tracks
I know they're not alone.

Karaoke Night in the Underworld

This place is popping tonight, I whisper
to slumping souls ahead of me in line.
We've got nowhere else to be. I prefer
when they don't chat, simply wait for their time.

I rush, like a river, to the entrance.
The bouncer's eyes are ablaze and sinners
who have sinned too much lie in a semblance
of sleep; restless at his feet, no inner

peace. I set nickels on their drying tongues.
He guides me below and I hear bellows
shattering hearts. Orpheus has begun
to pour the mourning of a dove's sorrows

onto our ears. He was the wind, delight,
the sun's bright song and now he only croons
Nat King Cole's *Looking Back.* I know the sight
of her ghost turns him to salt when doubt looms,

but he is a great hero and poet.
So, are drinks on him tonight? You know it.

Stain My Skin

all day
in the aloe of the maguey.
Calmly
place your balmy
hands fresh
upon my searing flesh.

Say, "soothe."
Say sooth.

Tell me the secrets of the curanderos,
then I will cake herbs and mud on the heads of
arrows.
I am sharpening obsidian and feeling
the tips to pierce the shadows, which will start the
healing

process.

Sitting in St. Ferdinand's,

my hands
fell asleep
under my thighs,
against the cold
wood of the old,
church pews.
The choir croons
its final exaltation
but we can't leave
until the father
drags his feet
from the altar
that rests
below
the gilded cross,
through the nave
and its
parted sea
of people
floating with arms
in the air.

Outside
the sun beams
brilliant
and the congregation
chirps
but that does not
have my attention.

I am focused.
I can smell my goal
waiting for me
across the street.
The cozy aroma
of bread,
just pulled
from the oven,
is calling my name
from the corner.
I tug
on my mother's blouse,
pointing
toward the only
reason
I sat through an hour
and a half
of lecture
and homily.
The only thing
that can revivify
my tingling
fingers.

Panaderia San Fernando,
where culture and history
is baked
into every crumb
and fed
into the waiting mouths

of the meek
who transform
into saints,
only for
a moment.
Where sins
absolve themselves
once you bite
into the warmth
of that soft,
fresh pan.
Where holy water
is the drool
from the sides
of our mouths,
as it blesses
our faces.

Trays upon trays
of rainbows
of conchas
brighten the room.
Tortugas bathe
in the white sands
of crystalized
sugar.
Puerquitos roll
in ginger
and butter
and spice.

The bible
mentioned heaven
but I didn't think
I'd be allowed
to visit here
weekly.
The miracle is real
and I can nearly
taste it.

A brown bag
is stuffed,
the paper
bursting
with our treats
for the week.
On the ride home
I am overjoyed,
for when I sit
in the dining room
I will baptize
mi elote
en leche,
spilling the sacrament
on the table.

I will sing
hallelujah
with a full mouth,
every word
will be heard.
And I will clasp
my hands together
in prayer.

Never Hide

Be proud of what you are.
The world needs to see
your steady, blood-brushed arm
planting bullets like seeds

into brown and black heads.
How are you the boys in blue
if all you leave behind is red?
It seems you already knew

your sins couldn't be washed
away with any water,
whether it was boiling or not.
We mourn another daughter,

mother, woman, queen.
No, we can't trust you to police us.
Believe that I say what I mean,
"I rebuke you in the name of Jesus."

Dear Elpenor,

When you fell,
your soft, yellow
bones cracked
the glass sky.
I could tell
thunder's bellow,
with a lone flash
of blurred light,

carried the sound
to unflinching stone,
a cold, resting place,
a fitting tomb.
In life, you drowned
deep and alone,
misremembering your face
as it lost its youth.

Empty amphora
shattered at your feet,
as blood and wine
swiftly spill a fresh dawn
upon the white sands of Aeaea.
Days elapsed below the heat,
the sun is felt divine.
An odyssey continues on.

The body ceases to shiver;
old, broken remains
begin to heal.
Another bright beginning shone,
on blue lips delivered;
a new refrain
to sing with zeal.
Warrior, return home.

From the gods, a second chance is handed;
please, Elpenor, don't take it for granted.

Reverse Nervous

Turn back the clock from twelve 'til we're one.
It won't wash the blood but shows, we've begun
Turn back the clock from twelve 'til we're one.
When injustice is law, resistance will come.

Wine into paper cups
with the page of cups.
Pulling leaves from adjacent brush,
it's sacred stuff.
Coalesce into vapor puffs, the day combusts.
"A spirit is ageless dust,
yes." The sages grunt.

Summon the shaman who speaks with stars,
Recording messages on an old VCR
We'll meet on Mars in a local tiki bar.
He's got freaky scars and he breathes so hard....
he says:

"I see behind me
The sea reminding
What dreams are finding
A realigning
Of seams unwinding
While teeth are grinding,
The streets igniting
That seems exciting.

In famished flames, there falls art devoured
Time trudges ticks in armless hour,
Realization sits on our hearts soon sour
The truest illusion is harmless power. "

Turn back the clock from twelve 'til we're one.
It won't wash the blood but shows, we've begun
Turn back the clock from twelve 'til we're one.
Your justice is flawed; we'll rise with the sun.

Mictēcacihuātl,

an innocent Lily rests in your hands.
Swallow the stars, so she can rise in day-
light. Open your palms, let her paint the sands
to match the color of her heart. Delay

the dark, leave a fire dancing, igniting
so, she can bake cookies and cinnamon
rolls. She's fearless and never stops fighting,
always wearing that smile which warms the sun.

Her favorite is jasmine green tea, please
constantly have a cup ready for her
to drink. Wash her of the mourning and leave
no suffering in her eyes. For on earth,

she had endured more than anyone should,
but no illness could diminish her glow.
She'd laugh, crack jokes, and truly understood:
life is beautiful and we all should know.

Send ladybugs to rest on the petals
of lilies. I will prepare the kettle.

42 | I Still Worship the Sun

East and West

A burgeoning blue
breathes
upon a new
sky.
Driving sunset bound
on the 10,
under the gold
of Nanahuatzin's
eye,
a humble bird martyrs
itself into my windshield.

Sometimes
the universe
likes to paintbrush
in crimson.
Sometimes
god's crystal tears
can't cleanse the sin
of cracked glass
and wine-soaked
feathers
dripping young
sacrament
into the hungry maw
of an impatient engine.

Broken wings
point east to west
in highway crucifixion.
A sacrifice
of claw
and body
and song.
I held
the unholy
rose-colored
shards in my
jaw.

I wore
shattered skin.
I drank
the exhaust
from the stained air,
It billowed
in my lungs
until my vision
became fractured
ripples
on a flooded lake
where the innocent
drown.

I couldn't speak
only a dirge
hummed from my
chewed lips.
I'll never hear
the chorus chime
from a sparrow's throat,
for it is forbidden
apocrypha.
I'll never feel
the freedom flight offers,
as I am
anchored by guilt,
shackled in jade,
weighed down
by the plumes.

Each
fragmented prism,
swimming
in my mouth,
solely refracted black
when I cried that night
because I knew
I'd have to chase
the sunrise.

II.
I Drink Tea Now

48 |

The Perfect Tea

I will learn everything I need
to brew the perfect tea
and recognize each
by the color of their leaves;

their exposure to the golden sun,
their floral scents that fill my lungs
with petals and their blooming buds.
The stems I hold will soon become

dry in warm hands that crave
your lips' tender touch. I praise
the sweetness of your taste
after you've had a cup. Days,

nights, and each morning I will pour your tea
because you love it and you are everything to

50 | I Drink Tea Now

I Met an Artist from Pomona
(previously published in Inlandia: A Literary Journal vol. 14)

an amaranth ember
dancing at the tip
of lit sage

cleansing, gracious spirit
coated in paint
alabaster hands of clay

in the waves of burning
hearts and the breath
of gleaming days

dreams are scrawled
on walls, as the drums
of golden footsteps pave

when we touch we're
immortal and while
I'm in her blaze

it feels that way

Two Statues in a Garden

Your hands are covered in paint and clay
from what you create each day.
That's okay,
that's okay.
I prefer it that way.

While our fingers are interlaced
I feel sculpted together in embrace
That's okay,
that's okay.
I prefer it that way.

My Eyes Caught You and I Thought

She can unbraid my hair
A tangle of timelines
She can unbraid this fear
Strangled by hindsight

Well, where do I begin?
Let's set the mood right
While amongst my kin
I drip in moonlight

Now here, this some fucking honest shit.
I waltzed into your life, asking who's your favorite
novelist
Bolaño, Morrison, or are you on that Austen-ish?
Absorbed by your godliness, I will be your audi-
ence.

Mi reina…

kisses language down my languid throat.
Tongues of burning passion lash in sacred oath
The past is vast and basks in naked prose
Alas, we outlast steadfast in face of ghosts

Parade in air,
angle for limelight.
We're made to err
mangle the guidelines

So, where does it end?
Impending doom, right?
Well, until then
I'll sip your moonlight.

Darjeeling

Amber pond tranquil
golden glow of afternoon
exquisite, soft touch

Early Grey

Sour fruit's nectar drips
into the waiting mouths of
old nobility

English Breakfast

Blended darkness in
warm hands will be fed to sky
to wake a new sun

Wild Chamomile

Hands guillotine full
beautiful blossoms, dry heads
find you rest each night

Silver Needle

Young leaves elegant
rare white blades dance energized
striking new morning

Ginger

Root yourself in earth
Fill life with spice, begin to

Oolong
Dark dragon breathes in
beams under a strong sun to
bless its withered leaves

Sencha

Petals from fallen
roses float sweetly on light's
delicate surface

Matcha

Flourishing in cool
shade brings fine, bright, and verdant
powder to restore

Snapping
(previously published in The Chaffey Review vol. 13)

frail necks fresh from birth;
feeling the thorns'
sharp kiss and shallow breath
haunt my skin.

I encase the blossoms
in a glass grave,
allowing their delicate,
florid petals to prostrate

and their pure perfume
to decay. As beauty wades
in clear tomb,
I hand you these slumping

symbols of fading life
in romantic gesture.

How to Train a Tiger

He traveled with the circus.
Dark scars
climbed up
his wide arms
like ladder rungs.

He said the trick to training a tiger
is to not control her,
but let her live free.
He dreams every day
of opening each cage
and throwing away the key.

Our First Kiss Lies in the Spring of Yesterday

The mariposas have migrated from
the pit of my trembling stomach and flown
up to my fluttering mouth,
lathering my tongue in leftover
nectar, so you can drink the tea from
the flowers bathing in my words.

I shower you in marigolds and soft,
orange wing beats, gentle on
the breeze. A gift fitting of a monarch.

My Love Language is

discussing how we'll change the world
with art.
Using
sculpture, painting, and the written word
will start
a spark
to bloom a blaze.

I love when you see a fence littered
with sores of rust or a wall with weathered,
cracked skin, you imagine how colors will
swirl upon their broken frame.

A sapphire blue, on a building's beaten husk,
can reach into the ancient dust
to pull a crumbling empire from a sunken dream
to its former glory.

Or how a honeyed gold on lamp posts
can once again make pyramids glow
under the sun's
scorching gaze.

Or how jade on gnarled, iron bars
summons the wind serpent
to bestow knowledge on those
who press its brilliant feathers
to their yearning heads.

My love language is starting an ever-burning fire
with you
that will wash the world in our heat and light.

My favorite sexual position is revolutionary.

III.

Family Fables

66 |

See Ya', Sofia

"Fuck. Where is that social worker's number?"
I tear through kitchen drawers. Pulling them out of
their holes,
leaving them to dangle like dry, wagging tongues.
"Her number is here, I know it is." I need her to
know, so that everything is finalized.

Knots of silver-plated jewelry rope my wrists to the
past
and I can't get to the hospital in time.
"Where is her fucking number!?" Where is it?
I knock more dents into the trash can,
as it spills onto the floor, spitting out messy secrets
and half-empty containers of freezer-burned meals.
On my knees, I begin to sort through credit card
offers, final notices,
and ripped pamphlets from clinics...
What if I can't find it? What if...

I-I can explain everything...
Lies lie like lumps in my throat, trying to convince
myself,
scraping the tips of fingers over the chipped stone
of my wedding ring.
Old gold band wrapped around a young brass heart.
He loves me, he'll understand,
and he'll forgive. Honey, I thought about you every
day.
I sung your name on the nights I was most lonely.

I carved your initials on the bleeding backs of fleet-
ing lovers.
I wanted you with me. And I know we could be a
family,
a real family with him.

Taking photos at Sears.
Imagine how beautiful, the three of us.
Soil-skin woman, soil-skin baby, white man,
in a red mask of boozy bliss, at center. We'd wear
matching yellow outfits
and matching wide, yellow smiles while the tired,
gray photographer
tries to match our enthusiasm, feebly attempting to
grab our son's attention.
Just stay still for a single second, mijo.
Please, to capture this perfect moment of familial
bliss forever.
Imperfection coats my tongue, dripping into the
shape of sentences,
with my coupon I clipped this morning, we'd only
have to pay $79.99
for the framed package deal!
Which is a steal and a half.
And he could be half yours.

But honey, I know you'll say no
because he isn't your son and because you'll never
know of his existence.
If you did, you'd leave drooling wounds in the
wall,
crimson mouths aghast as you make your exit,
to never look at us again.
When only a phone receiver and a wall of thick
glass separates us,
I feel you still can't see me.
On the other side of iron bars, I'm invisible but not
safe.
And that's okay... that's okay...
because I love you
and he's a dream that can't come true.

"Where is that fucking social worker's number?"

My Mother is a Hummingbird

Surrounded by warped wooden bars, I awake on a pile of glass bottles, syringes, and rusted curettes. It was a bed she once slept on in a past life. From the cracks of blinds, the dawn's orange glow slithers over the sterile white room and onto my crooked face to open my eyes. Hapless tripping on the capless bottles, in an attempt to stand, the liquor spills, staining half my body as the smell burns my nose. Eventually, I am able to stumble to my feet to the sounds of loud clinks, where surgical instruments and liquor bottles waltz.

The only décor in the room shakily whirls above my head – a farce of a mobile. A teetering halo of bent wire coat hangers, with arms limply holding gold-plated nickel rings. The cubic zirconia on each, dimly reflects the sun's light. I unwrap the wire from one, cutting my finger in the process, bleeding on the synthetic. I drop the ring in a shallow bottle, watching the clear liquid blush, and I take them both with me.

I jump to reach the top of the wooden bars, with a fingertip grip slowly slipping off. My feet are chewed as I land on the freshly fractured glass and I take a moment to pick the chipped teeth from my soul. I climb again, left with handfuls of splinters after each reach—palms on the summit, I lift my weight and shift it towards freedom, sliding down onto the cold tile below.

On the doorway, drab, grey curtains drape

to the floor. With the bottle dragging by my side, I crawl on my stomach desperate to make my exit. I pull back the curtains and the early sun greets me with a blinding hello. The smell of freshly turned dirt and dry grass join in the chorus of the greeting. The sallow turf is coarse and rough on my feet as I leave footprints of blood on my way to the flower bed.

It is barren with holes recently sunk. It better resembles small graves for small animals rather than a home for beautiful blooms. Yet I am determined. From the pockets of my navy, blue uniform shorts, I procure seeds of sunsets. Brushing my shaggy hair to the side, I dig my hands into the warm soil, sewing my hopes of seeing you into the heart of the earth. Off to the side a sack of sugar and an old, dented watering can wait in the dirt. The weather-beaten can is filled with stale-smelling, brown water. However, you and it are all I have. So, I use it. I have to leave, but I say to the mound of dirt, "Wait for me because I'll wait my whole life for you."

I'm riding the bus. The kids around me are singing songs or reciting jokes their parents taught them. I try to block this out because I want you singing to me and you telling me these jokes to be the first time I hear them. I like to pretend I know what your favorite color is; I assume it's red. I've planned the day that you come to see me countless times in my head: We'll tour my garden I made for

72 | Family Fables

you, I'll make mac n' cheese in the microwave and
pour you a glass of sugar water, we'll talk about
all the time we've lost and our conversations will
be seamless like none was lost at all, then I'll play
your favorite cassette tapes (you'll have to tell me
who your favorite artists are when you visit) and
we'll dance to them until the sun hides behind the
mountains and the moon lights the sky.

     The teacher is a young woman, I think in her
late twenties. I once called her "mom" and all the
kids in the class shook their desks, erupting in bois-
terous laughter. Although, I was not embarrassed,
I was ashamed. No matter how smart or kind she
is to me, there is no way that she could compare to
you. I pore through an encyclopedia, consuming
all the information I can regarding the subject of
hummingbirds, as the teacher orates her lessons.
While admiring a particularly beautiful picture
of a Fiery-throated Hummingbird, I imagine the
warmth of your voice. How its beauty would sing
comfort onto my head after a rough day at school.
How everything would be okay in that moment and
the eternity after. The teacher raises her soft voice,
calling my attention back to the history lesson.
Today she was discussing the Civil War and how in
this bloody conflict brothers killed brothers. I didn't
have any siblings I knew of, so I couldn't relate to
this but maybe they did exist. And maybe one day
I'd find them and maybe we'd disagree on which
one of us was truly your favorite and maybe they

would try to kill me or maybe I would kill them. With clammy hands, I slam the encyclopedia closed and walk out of the classroom, leaving the school. I hop on my bike with broken spokes and ride home. Hoping to find life, hoping to find you.

I am elated when I arrive to see that the seeds have sprouted. Thin green sinews reaching out from beneath the dirt in a futile attempt to touch the sun hanging in the middle of the sky. I grab the old can and see my reflection in the muddy water. It is unrecognizable. Short hair combed to the side above a gaunt face with tired eyes and a five o' clock shadow, and a red tie feebly choking me. Ignoring this stranger, I bash the head off the bottle by smashing it against a rock, then place the ring in my pant pocket. Grabbing the sack of sugar, I fill half the broken bottle and watch as it coalesces with the liquor and my blood. The bottle sits next to the budding plants as a sentry, guarding them for the rest of its life. I check my watch and notice that my lunch break is almost over. Before I leave, I water the sprouts and say to them, "She'll come for you, but she'll stay for me."

My car wears scraped sides, three different shades of grey on the doors, and dents on the hood. It was lunch hour traffic, I was catching every red light, and this brought a smile to my face. I drove into the parking structure, passing endless rows of the same models and colors of cars. Black and white and red and black and white and red. Finally,

I reach the peak, just below the hanging afternoon sun, and pull into my designated spot. Realizing how late I was, I ran down the stairs and through the business park plaza. Trampling through bushes and dirt, I stop at the Black-eyed Susans. They are watching me without judgement. Their bright, yellow petals, encircling dark eyes, are calling my name. I approach and snap one's neck, holding the flower's head between my fingertips. I continue to the building, climbing up the stairs and sneaking into my seat.

Eschewing monotonous work, I often draw pictures of hummingbirds, imagining how you look. The blues and greens swirled around but your throat, where the beautiful songs were birthed, burned bright oranges and reds. I stand, peeking my head over the cube and hand the dilapidated flower, bent at the stem, with missing petals, to my cubicle neighbor and say, "This reminded me of you." We always share pithy remarks. For example, today she responded with, "Did you just pick this from outside?" I shrug my shoulders and wryly look around the mundane office and out the windows. She adds, "You smell of sweat, alcohol, and dirt." To which I wittily reply, "I think you are cute too." This continues as endlessly as typing on this computer in this grey box feels; fluorescent bulbs hum forever. We share our last break together. I finally ask, "You should come over after work to meet my mother." I show her the picture I drew. "She should be home by then." She ruminates on this but eventually smiles and agrees. We leave, walking by the trampled bushes and the Black-eyed Susans bowing their heads at us or the sun. I'm never sure which.

When we arrive at the bed, I am amazed at how much the flowers have grown. Tall stalks with budding, exuberant heads nodding in the wind. I grab the old, dented watering can then fill the bottle with sugar and blood. "Soon the brilliant bloom will be here and so will my mother," I say. She grasps my hand in hers, we sit in dirt and wait. I pull the ring from my pocket and slide it onto her finger. She accepts it and rests her head on my shoulder.

The bloom is full and bears the brightest red and orange I have ever seen. Deep and vibrant petals that challenge the beauty of the sun. They truly are the most perfect of Daylilies to welcome you home. In our elation, we put on cassette tapes and dance around the flowers. We dance for years and years but you never come. We wait and wait but you never show. She tells me, "It's okay, let's go inside, it'll be night soon." I decline and sit in the dirt. She decides to sit back down with me. We wait for something that will never occur. She gets up a few times, plays the cassette tapes, and tries to convince me to dance again. However, I decline and continue to water the flowers until the handle of the rusted watering can breaks off. I hear a buzzing from the sack of sugar to find that flies have feasted on what remains, leaving their eggs and larvae swimming through the crystals. I sit back down and watch as the sun begins its descent into the crown of mountains. She sits and waits longer than expected but eventually smiles, shakes her head, and says, "I can't do this anymore." She releases my hand from her caring grip, takes off the ring, drops it into my splintered palms and leaves.

I wait for decades and you never come. I throw the ring into the street. I stomp on the old watering can, I smash the bottle over the flowers, and I empty the sack of maggots over the soil. I rip the head off the Daylilies and bury them in the warm dirt. The day is ready to retire and so am I. And as the sun finishes setting, I watch the gold wash over me.

Hand-Me-Down

Praise be!
I have finally found religion
in that bible with the dilapidated spine
slumping next to my empty glass.

I have definitely found religion
in those glint-less, gold-trimmed pages
which lay slumped near my replenished glass.
If only I could open that book.

The indistinct glint-less, gold-trimmed pages
are obscured in this room by charcoal walls and
dark-brown furniture.
I could never open the book.
I remember when you gave it to me, hoping that I'd
read it.

With disdain, I glare at the charcoal walls and dark-
brown furniture,
wishing that the walls would change to a more
pleasant color.
The day you handed it to me, you prayed that I'd
read it.
It was just a week before you passed.

Compared to dull charcoal, the powder blue hospi-
tal walls were a more pleasant color.
You said no matter what path in life I took, you'd
be proud.

That was just a week before you passed.
I brush a coat of dust off the book's leather skin.

No matter what path I traverse you'd always be
proud.
Where I choose to place my faith is my own deci-
sion, Abuelo.
Brushing even more dust off its leather skin,
I place my glass on the off-white cover.

I keep this tired book because I have faith in you,
Abuelo.
I glance again at that bible with the dilapidated
spine.
My glass resting on its off-white cover.
My religion is submerged in this clear, light-brown
liquid. Praise be.

Mom's Kitchen

always had the drab, sun-soaked yellow
curtains pulled aside.
So, that the window would
allow light to pour into the room,
illuminating and focusing
on the decrepit oven.
That shoddy piece of junk
hardly ever worked.

She fiddled with the fickle knobs
trying to ignite
the machine, so she could continue
preparing dinner for us.
I believe she was crafting
her green enchiladas,
my favorite.
It was an old family recipe
that had been passed down
through several generations.

She had been so tired, lately.
Struggling to raise a child on her own
after her husband had left to the other side of the
country
to found himself a younger woman.
My mother exhaustively queried her fatigued re-
flection
in the glass of the window,
"What does she have that I don't?

Why does he love her more than me?"
To which she never received a reply.

And now the damned, burnt-out oven refused to
cooperate.
Nothing in her life seemed to go according to plan.
The weight of all that had recently occurred
had proven to be too much
as she fell
silent on the floor.
With shallow breaths and blank eyes,
she lied there.
Lady, concerned with the commotion,
heard the noise and entered
from the compact hole in the door that led to the
backyard.
She gently nuzzled
my mother's hand,
with her cold snout,
anticipating a response.
There was none.

She rested her head against my mother's,
exhaling only when she inhaled.
The light had left
when I inserted my key into the lock
and twisted.

Constellations

You are the first woman I loved.

I remember those frigid nights
I was about five
or six.
The cold would seep through my skin,
grasp at my bones and squeeze
at my starving lungs. The air on those
nights, transformed my breath
into constructs of clouds, forming
semblances of dogs,
birds, and your grey 91' Honda Accord
that we used to ride in
everywhere.

Just you and me, adventuring
with the sun at our back. Driving
the only destination being
our happiness. You always tried
your best to make me smile,
and I usually did, but rarely
on those frigid nights.
Those nights where the ambiguous
shapes I made blended
with your smoke to create something
completely different.

There you were sitting on the front
porch, all by yourself, crying,

wondering if dad would ever return
to join our fractured family
again.
Crying and smoking cigarettes.
Those slender sticks
held by yellowed fingertips
carried multiple forms of cancer,
including but not limited to,
the cancer of his memory.
Those were his
brand of cancer.

That stupid white box
with its green trimmings,
bent corners, and battered
edges. He always carried
that box and he always
had one lit; sucking up
the fumes, like a dying fish
desperate for water, then expelling
a toxic haze that shadowed
his steps everywhere he went.
I had asthma, but he didn't
seem to mind. Occasionally,
he would tell me to stop
coughing as he couldn't hear
his oldies over the sounds
of my struggled breathing,
I'm Your Puppet blared
on car speakers,
but other than that, he didn't

seem to mind at all.

But there you were, sitting
on those cold, concrete steps
during those even colder nights
when you felt most alone.
A suddenly single mother, struggling
to raise her son, longing
for what you've lost. It wasn't
the cigarettes you craved
those nights.
It was the cancer
that was him
and this was the only way
you felt you could savor
a taste. Maybe because
it was reminiscent
of the tar in his kiss
or that the nicotine had permanently
seeped into his dry,
cracked lips and whenever
he spoke you became more addicted.

With the cigarette clutched
by the pursing of your lips,
the smoke crawled
into your body and caressed
your soul. You were hoping
to blacken your lungs to match
the night's sky,

to match his heart.
I sat next to you breathing
in the memories of him
that you've created,
and in that moment,
that hung in the air
forever, I pointed out
that the sky wasn't completely
black. The stars were visible,
shining with their otherworldly
glow. Flickering like a thousand
candles festooned across
the heavens, an eternity
of miles away.

Your tears reflected the light
of the stars
as you wiped them away.
You smashed the ember, sitting
at the end of his cancer, into
the cold concrete, extinguishing
it for now. Held in your arms,
I was warm; the cold's
grip had dissipated.

*There we were mother
and son, staring at the
canvas up high,
naming constellations.*

86 | Family Fables

Tonāntziné

When my mother told stories,
it was a construction zone.
The rumbles and the whirs
of her words
shook the room.
The dust kicked up,
by her enthusiastic hands
and feet, snowed
imagination onto my head.

She stacked brick onto brick as she built worlds.
She carved myths into the waiting walls of my
dreams.
She planted seeds of our family's history at the
roots of my heels.
She nurtured those sprouts with her sweat and
tears.
She watched rustling leaves unfold into bustling
cities.
She harvested heroes that fruited from tall trees.
She protected the land with all of her being.

She showed me

       possibility,

      creativity,

       opportunity.

When my mother told stories,
I wore a hard hat,
stood a bit back, and listened.

| 89

Acknowledgements

There are many people who helped pull this book from the ether to its physical form and I am eternally grateful to each and every one of them. However, there is no one more responsible for this collection than my beautiful partner and muse, Janette Alejandra Lopez. When you entered my life, it was you who dragged me out of the writing rut I dug myself into. You encouraged me to go out there and start sharing my words with the world again. If it wasn't for you, I never would have found my confidence and none of this would be possible. So, for that I will thank you every day for inspiring me with your creativity, passion, and incredible art which has blessed this book. I love you. You can follow her art on IG @alejandra.studio.

Another tremendous source of inspiration throughout my life has been and always will be my parents. To my mother, thank you for being the reason I love stories. Your bedtime tales each night gifted me my love of writing. Your sense of humor helped form mine and your guidance and hard work taught me so much about life. To my father, you supported our family and always made me laugh. You taught me that about forgiveness and for that I am eternally grateful. Thank you both for being my parents.

I met Erica Castro at the 2024 Poetry Fest at the LA County Fair. I admired your poetry when I first heard it. Your passion for writing and spreading the love of poetry was apparent. Thank you for believing in me, my vision, and my work. You made the entire publishing process easier than I ever could have imagined. I am honored to have my work published by Daxson Publishing.

I must shout out my friends and LionLike family, Judah1 & Ces1. Your drive, your craft, your desire to enrich the world with your art, has inspired me in so many ways. Thank you for allowing me into the pride and helping me learn that poetry is more than just words. It's a community, it's family, and it continues thriving due in part to the amazing work you put in.

To my brothers in Pilgrimms, I love you. You are both brilliant and incredibly talented at what you do. Let's get in the lab soon and make some fire.

I appreciate every spot that has let me bless the mic: A Mic and Dim Lights, Barrio Fuerza, Creative Sounds, Obsidian Tongues, Whiskey and Words, and countless others. These are all sacred places and events that are so important and necessary for the community. Always support your local open mic.

Thank you to my beautiful friends for your constant support and understanding. You all are the realest and I am thankful every single day for you being in my life.

To the spirits of my ancestors, thank you for the stories passed down. You inspire me daily as the wind shaking leaves, as the sun giving life, as the mountains standing stoic on the horizon.

Lastly, I want to thank you the reader. Thank you for picking up this book, it is everything to me. Thank you for providing me the opportunity to share a bit of my story with you. I hope you find the opportunities to make your own myth.

94 |

About the Author

Peter Lechuga is a Mexican American poet, writer, teacher, musician, emcee, and karaoke king born and raised in Southern California. As director of LionLike Creative Education, he teaches future generations the power of poetry, while creating a safe space for them to express themselves, find their own voice, and become published authors. He makes anti-capitalist, anti-colonial hip-hop with the avant-garde art collective Pilgrimms, whose tunes can be found anywhere you stream music. His poetry has been shared on college campuses and has been published in the Chaffey Review, Inlandia Institute, Spoiled Minds amongst other publications. When not reading, writing, or killing the mic, he can be found hiking in the mountains, spitting freestyles. Follow his journey on IG @handsomeherbivore

Publisher's Note

Daxson publishing was created to help marginalized artists publish their work, so the world can hear their voice. The vision for this publishing house is to help people get their work out there, and not have them struggle finding their way through the publishing process. Everyone's voice deserves to be heard, and we are here to help. If you are interested in submitting a manuscript, email daxsonpublishing@gmail.com.